Introduction

CW01023382

Teignmouth is a popular seaside resort situated on the South Devon coast of England. Here the River Teign completes its journey from the high ground of Dartmoor to the English Channel. Since the Middle Ages the estuary of the River Teign has provided safe shelter and an opportunity for maritime trade including the export of locally quarried minerals. This trade has continued into the 21st Century and Teignmouth is still a busy port with around 150 ships calling each year.

The nearby Bovey Basin has one of the finest deposits of ball clay in the world. Following the successful development of manufacturing processes by potters such as Wedgwood and Spode, ball clay has been shipped from Teignmouth across the world for use in fine ceramic products. The opening of the Stover Canal in 1792 allowed barges to replace horse and wagons to transport clay to Teignmouth for transshipment to sea going vessels. The opening of the Haytor Tramway in 1820 allowed Dartmoor granite to be delivered to the canal basin at Ventiford for onward movement by barge. Granite shipped through Teignmouth has been used in the construction of many famous structures including the original London Bridge, the British Museum and Buckingham Palace.

Whilst many small ports have closed since the 1980s the demand for ball clay has allowed Teignmouth to remain economically viable. Ball clay is exported from Teignmouth across Europe and North Africa for the manufacture of ceramic white ware. The port also supports other local industry with inbound cargoes of fertilizer, animal feed, road salt, ground granulated blast furnace slag and road stone. Infrastructure projects also increasingly use the quays to load equipment or bunker vessels and Teignmouth's fishing fleet is still very active.

As the country moves towards a carbon neutral economy the port offers South Devon the environmental benefits of sea transport. A ready example is each ship from Port Talbot, South Wales carrying ground granulated blast furnace slag for use in the production of concrete removes around 70 lorry loads from the M4 and M5 motorways.

In the competitive world of transport, ship owners and shippers need the benefits of economies of scale and the draft of ever larger vessels brings challenges for Teignmouth. Competition for trade has also increased from the port at Plymouth, which benefits from being able to handle larger vessels than Teignmouth. Fortunately, investment in the port facilities at Teignmouth has continued with over £5m spent in recent years increasing the channel depth, introducing new material handling equipment and developing warehousing on the quays.

My interest in the port started as a child watching the comings and goings. I was always fascinated about the strange names on the sterns of the ships and the distant destinations. This interest was a big influence in my career and for the last 30 years I have never been far away from ships and ports. When I returned to Devon in 2015, I was keen to record the modern-day shipping scene and this book was initially a COVID-19 lock down project of the best of my recent photographs. On showing the self-printed result to friends I was persuaded to see if it could be published and, despite my initial

reservations, I was very pleased t
Shipping agreed it was a worthwhile project.

At the time of completing the initial book it was unimaginable the sights the global pandemic would bring in the second half of 2020. The adjacent Babbacombe Bay has always provided shelter but for over twelve months some of the finest passenger ships in the world, including the last operational ocean liner *Queen Mary 2*, laid up off Teignmouth awaiting the recommencement of international travel. To cover this fascinating period the original scope has been increased to include the waters between neighbouring Dawlish and Maidencombe. The luxury visitors also brought more interest in the local shipping scene with the 'Ships in Torbay and Lyme Bay' Facebook group now having an incredible 21,000 followers.

During the relatively short period of time covered by this publication there has been significant change in the vessels serving Teignmouth. Carrying capacity has increased with 5,000 tonne payload ships now common whilst many older and smaller vessels have moved away from Northern Europe to the Mediterranean or further afield. Some ships have been scrapped and some lost. The UK also left the European Union but it so far appears to have had little impact on cargo volumes at the port.

Thank you to the late Bernard McCall for not only taking on this book but spending three decades producing publications that proved invaluable to both professionals and enthusiasts. Bernard's work widened knowledge and interest in the short-sea shipping scene when the subject was generally ignored by mainstream publishers. My copy of the bimonthly Coastal Shipping magazine was passed around the office with colleagues amazed with the useful information on new vessels, port activity and cargo movements. Thank you to Iain McCall for continuing the project in such unfortunate and unexpected circumstances.

Thank you to the members of the World Ship Society for providing so much information on the local shipping scene and thanks to Hugh Rodway for producing his excellent weekly blog on West Country shipping movements. Thank you to Malcolm Fletcher and Tom Walker for proofreading the book and providing plenty of constructive feedback. Recognition is particularly required for my long-suffering daughters Matilda and Bea. At least you were never late for school when there was an early tide and hopefully the ice creams, hot chocolates and trips to Shaldon Bakery were some compensation for having to hang around on the beach in all weathers. Thank you, girls.

For reference I have used three excellent books that I can recommend for anyone wanting to know more about the port and its cargoes. These are *Teignmouth* by HJ Trump, *The Ball Clays of Devon and Dorset* by the Ball Clay Heritage Society and *Haytor Granite - A Celebration* by Stuart Drabble.

For each ship I have shown the year built and the payload capacity as summer deadweight tonnes (DWT) for cargo ships and gross tonnes (GT) for passenger ships.

On 2nd October 1993 the Teignmouth dredger *Tarway* is moored alongside the Sand Quay. As the name suggests, *Tarway* started life as a tar barge on the Solent and was built in 1958 by Fairmile Shipyard (Berwick) Ltd. The vessel kept the channel clear at Teignmouth for many years and delivered sand to the quay from where it was sold for use in construction. When dredging operations were taken over by the new Teignmouth Harbour Commissioners tug *Teign C* the familiar red barge left Teignmouth to operate again on the Solent, this time as an aggregate carrier. Once withdrawn from commercial traffic the barge moved onto Maldon, Essex where the name was modified to *Starway*. From 2011 the well-travelled vessel was converted to a four-bedroom luxury home and in early 2022 was for sale in Brentford, West London for £260,000 with the original name restored.

In April 2012 the Polish owned **Poprad** (1986, 1,980DWT) makes a fine sight entering the Teign estuary. The Poprad is a river in northern Slovakia and southern Poland with a length of 170 kilometres. Now named **My Efekan 2** the ship has swapped the Baltic for the warmer climate of the Eastern Mediterranean. The Point at Teignmouth is a popular location to watch ships making the 90 degree turn into the port and my father and eldest daughter get a fine view of the German built ship. To photograph moving ships the light is best in the morning on the Teignmouth side and from late morning the Shaldon side of the estuary offers the best opportunities. Fortunately the main quays are south facing so can be photographed from various locations throughout the day. To get across the Teign there are a number of options including the historic ferry service or via Shaldon Bridge by road or foot.

On 3rd August 2013 reserve RNLI inshore Atlantic 85 lifeboat B-803 **William Hurst** (2005) was preparing to stand-by at the Shaldon Water Carnival procession when it was tasked to assist an eight metre pleasure boat off Langstone Rock, Dawlish. The boat with four adults on board was taken in tow to Exmouth Marina. Whilst leaving the Marina, a jet ski with two adults and a child was observed in difficulties by the lifeboat crew. The jet ski was then towed to the Exmouth Marina slipway. The Atlantic 85 is 8.5 metres long and named after Atlantic College in Wales where these rigid inflatable lifeboats were first developed. Introduced in 2005 the Atlantic 85 is the third generation of B Class lifeboat replacing the Atlantic 75 which in turn had replaced the Atlantic 21, which first entered service in 1972.

On 27th October 2014 the Bijlsma Shipyard in Lemmer, Netherlands built *Virage* (2012, 3,200DWT) departs from Teignmouth with a cargo of ball clay. The Bijlsma Trader 3250 class vessel has since transferred port of registration from Werkendam, Netherlands to London and now carries the name *Eastern Virage*. Teignmouth was recorded as a port by the 14th Century and developed a major role in the Newfoundland cod fishing trade. In July 1690 Teignmouth was raided by the French with this being the last recorded invasion of the English mainland. Various minerals, coal, food stuffs, granite, timber and even cider were handled at the port but ball clay became the stable export with the first shipment being recorded in the early 18th Century. The availability of a reload made Teignmouth an attractive port for shipowners and the Stoke-on-Trent pottery industry was a major destination for the Bovey Basin clay. With the demise of significant china production in the United Kingdom it is now mainland Europe and North Africa that are the destinations of cargoes leaving Teignmouth.

On 4th May 2015 the **Swift** (1989, 1,400DWT) leaves Teignmouth in ballast for Rouen. This vessel is a Yorkshire Dry Dock Economy Coaster known by many for obvious reasons as a YDD Box. Built in Hull the design was popular with British owners and a common sight in Teignmouth from the 1980s until the mid-2010s. Launched as the **Hoo Swift** the vessel was yard no.318 and has not traded since 2016. Of the 14 YDD coasters built to a length of 58 metres only the **River Trader**, the former **Hoo Beech** is still trading in Northern Europe.

On 17th May 2015 the **Jade** (2010, 3,261DWT) arrives at Teignmouth from Rotterdam. The vessel is another Bijlsma Trader 3250 built in Lemmer, Netherlands and is registered in Amsterdam. It is described by the builders as a true multipurpose vessel with strengthened tank tops to carry heavy loads and a container capacity of 104 TEU containers.

On 16th June 2015 the **Fluvius Axe** (1998, 3,193DWT) arrives at Teignmouth from Fowey to top up a clay cargo. Launched as the **Arklow Sea** by the Barkmeijer Shipyard, Stroobos, Netherlands, the vessel is owned and managed by Exe Shipping of Powderham, Devon. All vessels in the fleet are named after Devon rivers with Fluvius being Latin for river, stream or running water and the Axe a 22 mile river which enters Lyme Bay between Axmouth and Seaton. The beach at Shaldon is an ideal location to combine both a paddle with watching the shipping movements around high tide. The website of shipping agents Pike Ward Ltd has a very useful list of many of the planned movements although weather delays can impact on schedules. Movements usually take place in the hour before high water and there are generally more ships during spring tides.

On 22nd July 2015 the **Hebridean Princess** (1964, 2,112GT) is seen leaving Teignmouth for Portland towards the end of a cruise from Oban. This was the first visit of a large passenger ship to Teignmouth since the Victorian era and was welcomed by the press and residents. Built as the **Columba** by Hall, Russell & Company, Aberdeen for the Secretary of State for Scotland it was one of a trio of car ferries chartered to David MacBrayne Ltd to serve the Western Isles. Once withdrawn from ferry service the vessel was refitted at Great Yarmouth in 1989 for the luxury cruise market and renamed the **Hebridean Princess**. In 2006 and 2010 Her Majesty the Queen chartered the vessel for holiday cruises in Scottish waters.

On 3rd October 2015 the Hull built and London registered **Falcon** (1991, 2,200DWT) approaches Teignmouth from Ipswich. The vessel is a larger version of Yorkshire Dry Dock Economy Coaster and at the time was operated by British company Absolute Shipping which unfortunately ceased trading in 2016. The vessel is now the Panamanian registered **Alcon** and is operating in the Eastern Mediterranean and Black Sea.

On 23rd November 2015 the *Russa* (1980, 2,557DWT) is seen at Teignmouth loaded with ball clay for Ravenna, Italy. The *Hav Marlin* (1994, 3,046DWT) is to the right part loaded with ball clay. To the left is the stern of the *Swift* (1989, 1,400DWT) which had arrived earlier in the day with a cargo of potash from Teesport. The *Russa* was built as the *Baltiyskiy 110* by Wärtsilä, Turku, Finland and was owned at this time by Gotland Shipping, St. Petersburg, Russia. Once a common sight in Teignmouth this may well prove to be the last visit by one of this class of standard Russian river-sea ships. The vessel was scrapped in Turkey in 2016.

On the morning of 29th December 2015 the *Frem Nordica* (1986, 1,601DWT) arrives at Teignmouth from Klaipeda, Latvia with a cargo of calcium ammonium nitrate fertilizer. Built in 1986 by Peters Shipyard, Kampen, Netherlands the Danish registered ship was at the time owned and managed by Jmb Bjerrum & Jensen, Svendborg, Denmark. In January 2020 the vessel was reregistered in Panama with the name *Hoop* but this didn't last long as in October 2021 the name *SNP Sun* was adopted under the flag of Vanuatu with the vessel operating in the Mediterranean.

On 3rd February 2016 the **Celtica Hav** (1984, 1,720DWT) ran aground on The Point at Teignmouth whilst arriving in ballast from Avonmouth. The entrance to Teignmouth is particularly challenging with a tight turn and strong currents. Fortunately, events such as this are very rare and quick work by the pilot boat on the bow and the harbour tug **Teign C** on the stern saw the **Celtica Hav** on her way after a short delay.

On 7th March 2016 the Bodewes Shipyard, Netherlands built **Ben Varrey** (1986, 1,546DWT) departs Teignmouth light for Marchwood. The coaster had delivered high polished stone value road stone from Belfast for use in asphalt. At the time the **Ben Varrey** was operated by Absolute Shipping, a British business which ceased trading shortly after this picture was taken. After layup in Rotterdam the classic coaster was sold to an operator in the Seychelles and since then has been trading in Chile as the **Logimar I**.

On 2nd April 2016 the **Serra Atasoy** (2011, 4,284DWT) swings at Teignmouth having arrived in ballast from Ellesmere Port on the Manchester Ship Canal. This first time Turkish caller loaded a cargo of ball clay. Now registered in Norway and named **Kryssholm** the vessel has been fitted with a crane and is operating in the Baltic. As is often seen the pilot boat **Syd Hook** provides assistance at the stern to help the vessel swing in the relatively narrow channel. In normal circumstances ships swing on arrival and moor port side to the wall.

On 20th April 2016 the **Nautica** (1992, 2,166DWT) arrives at Teignmouth from Antwerp in a swell caused by an easterly wind. The ship was launched as the **Vesting** at the yard of Ferus Smit in Westerbroek, Netherlands. The port pilot boat **Syd Hook** heads for some shelter in the estuary.

Sydney Hook was a senior pilot at the port for almost 25 years and in that time guided 10,000 ships in and out of port. In February 1985 he was awarded the British Empire Medal by the Duke of Edinburgh in a ceremony at Trinity House for services to pilotage at Teignmouth. Syd was also awarded the Distinguished Service Medal for his service during the Second World War which included time on Landing Ship, Tank **LST403** on the Mediterranean front and at D-Day. **LST403** landed at Gold Beach under enemy fire to pick up the bodies of the dead and the wounded. In all they made six landings and seventeen trips between the English mainland and Normandy, bringing back thousands of troops and prisoners of war.

On 22nd May 2016 the *Jolie Brise* (1913) is welcomed to Teignmouth for the first time in 90 years. Launched in Le Havre she was the penultimate gaff-rigged cutter in pilot service before the change from sail to steam and the last boat to carry the Royal Mail under sail. Based at Teignmouth in the 1920s the vessel is now operated by Dauntsey School, Wiltshire and pupils from the school have sailed her across the Atlantic six times, crossed the Bay of Biscay 10 times, and navigated up to 200 miles inside the Arctic Circle. Named after France's equivalent of the Beaufort scale force five wind she has won the Fastnet Race three times, including the first race in 1925 when sailed by Teignmouth resident Sidney Briggs with Lieutenant Commander EG Martin OBE, founder of the Royal Ocean Yacht Club. More recently with Dauntsey's pupils on board she has been overall winner of the Tall Ships Races four times.

On 18th June 2016 the Danish split hopper dredger **Modi R** (1994, 734DWT) arrived at Teignmouth from Bremerhaven. The vessel was about to start a £250,000 dredging contract to deepen the entrance channel to allow higher capacity vessels to use the port. The vessel is named after the Nordic mythological son of Thor and in August 2021 was operating in Australia.

On 18th July 2016 the **Stefan K** (1995, 3,710DWT) departs from Teignmouth with a cargo of ball clay for Castellon, Spain. The harbour tug **Teign C** looked smart after a recent repaint in Plymouth and was acting as the pilot boat. The tug was built by Damen in the Netherlands to the Stan Tug 1405 design and is a very useful vessel being fitted for plough dredging and towage as well as being able to stand in for the pilot boat **Syd Hook** as required. The **Stefan K** is still trading in Northern Europe with Turkish management but has changed from the Dutch flag to Panamanian registration and renamed **Stefany**.

On 12th August 2016 the Dutch **Smaragd** (2003, 3,155DWT) arrives at Teignmouth from the River Tees. The vessel was built in the Netherlands by Barkmeijer Shipyard of Stroobos and at the time of the photograph owned by De Bock Maritiem BV of Alkmaar. The vessel is unusual in that throughout her career she has carried the same name which means 'Emerald' in Dutch. Designed by Conoship International BV of Groningen, Netherlands the vessel has a family likeness to Arklow ships from the same designer and builder, such as the former **Arklow Sea** seen on Page 7.

On 4th November 2016 the **RMS Goole** (2005, 2,620DWT) prepares to depart from Teignmouth for Loviisa Laicasilta, Finland. The fireworks display commemorating Guy Fawkes Night can be seen at Teignmouth Rugby Club.

On 8th February 2017 the diminutive **Eric Hammann** (1991, 1,323DWT) makes a fine sight arriving at Teignmouth from Rotterdam. This vessel along with three sister ships were built at 58 metres to navigate a tight turn in the River Trent which allowed the coasters to reach a wharf at Beckingham in Nottinghamshire. Unfortunately, the wharf has now closed and timber is transported by road from the Humber ports.

On 4th March 2017 the **Shetland Trader** (1992, 2,386DWT) arrives at Teignmouth to load sand for Guernsey. The vessel was built by Rosslauer Shipyard, Germany as the **Lass Mars** and is now in the fleet of Faversham Ships of East Cowes. This ship is still a regular sight in British waters serving many small ports including deliveries of barley to Port Ellen for use by the whisky distilleries of Islay. In 2017 there were at least two export cargoes of aggregates for Guernsey but unfortunately these have not been repeated.

On 10th May 2017 the **Celtic Crusader** (1994, 3,710DWT) arrives at Teignmouth in ballast. The Cardiff based Charles M. Willie (Shipping) Limited vessels are a regular sight in Teignmouth loading ball clay for Iberia. The company has a policy of replacing ships on a regular basis with good quality secondhand tonnage and the **Celtic Crusader** left the fleet in 2021 and is now trading in northern Europe as the **Rusader**.

On 10th May 2017 the **Nathalie** (1985, 1,529DWT) departs from Teignmouth for Guernsey with a cargo of aggregates. With a strong current and the wind against the elderly ship it is working hard to leave the estuary. This is the only picture in this book of a laden ship leaving Teignmouth with a cargo other than ball clay. Built as the **Werder Bremen** by Hermann Suerken GmbH of Papenburg, Germany the vessel is now trading in the Eastern Mediterranean as the **Seba**.

On 22nd May 2017 the **Aristote** (1983, 1,821DWT) departs from Teignmouth for Barry having delivered a cargo of road stone from Belfast. The low air draught river-sea ship was one of a class of four delivered to London and Rochester Trading Co. Ltd by Cochrane Shipbuilders of Selby, Yorkshire. The ships bore the names **Urgence**, **Vibrence**, **Stridence** and **Turbulence**. It was pleasing to see the former **Turbulence** still going strong 34 years after being launched into the River Ouse. As this is written the vessel is in Colombia and surprisingly trading again under the name of **Turbulence**. Teignmouth sees regular imports of road stone from Belfast for use in asphalt production. On higher risk sections of road such as junctions an asphalt is often specified with a greater resistance to skidding. The skid resistance capabilities of a stone is measured through the polished stone value (PSV) and Northern Ireland is one of the few areas that has quarries that produce stone with a higher PSV.

On 25th May 2017 the Terneuzen registered **Multrasalvor 3** (2012, 250DWT) arrives at Teignmouth whilst being used to support the Dawlish Warren beach replenishment project. A product of the Damen Shipyard at Hardinxveld, Netherlands the vessel is purpose built for civil engineering projects with a bollard pull of 27.8 tonnes, two cranes and an A-frame for dredging.

On the morning of 12th July 2017 the Dutch trailing suction hopper dredger **Mahury** (2016, 1,623DWT) arrives at Teignmouth. The vessel was being employed replenishing the beach at Dawlish Warren and probably calling at Teignmouth for bunkers. Built for Baggerbedrijf De Boer - Dutch Dredging by MTG Dolphin in Varna, Bulgaria the twin screw vessel is named after a river in French Guiana, South America, where the owner has a long-term contract for maintaining the depth of the approach to the seaport of Dégrad des Cannes.

On 4th September 2017 the **Bomar Moon** (2010, 2,803DWT) arrives at Teignmouth from Liepāja, Latvia on a perfect early autumn evening. Note the vessel's anchor is not fully stowed and is still in the water, an unusual sight. The German owned ship was built in Bangladesh but is now converted into a self-discharge vessel operated by Seaworks in Norway and named **Geir Tore H**.

On 11th January 2018 the Exeter registered cement carrier *Ronez* (1982, 1,117DWT) is seen arriving at Teignmouth with a cargo of ground granulated blast furnace slag (GGBS) from Port Talbot. This was a welcome visit to Teignmouth for the only Exeter registered deep sea vessel which was chartered to move GGBS for a number of months. Built by Scheepswerf van Goor Monnickendam BV, Monnickendam, Netherlands the self-pneumatic discharge vessel can carry 950 tonnes of cement. Owned by Ronez, the Channel Islands based supplier of construction materials, the vessel is regularly used to supply Guernsey and Jersey with cement and GGBS.

On 20th November 2017 the **Arklow Valley** (2016, 5,169DWT) and the **Kruckau** (2003, 3,683DWT) are seen at Teignmouth. The Port of Teignmouth is operated by Associated British Ports as part of a portfolio of 21 ports in the UK. In recent years £5 million has been invested in deepening the channel and the creation of 3,000 square metres of new transit sheds. This investment has been made to accommodate larger vessels and provide a significant improvement in ship turnaround times which keeps the port competitive. In 2021 the **Kruckau** was renamed the **Neckartal** but is still a familiar sight in northern Europe.

On 1st January 2018 the **Sea Hunter** (1990, 3,148DWT) is seen sheltering in Babbacombe Bay whilst en route from Brightlingsea, Essex to Pasajes, Spain. Launched as the **Sirrah** in Portugal the vessel is now trading in the Mediterranean under the Greek flag as **Anastasia K**. Behind are two ships waiting the tide to enter Teignmouth. The **Bekau** (2005, 3,701DWT) had travelled in ballast from Portbury. In 2020 the Slovakian built vessel transferred to the Faroe Island registry when renamed **Hav Westlandia**. The **Celtic Venture** (2002, 5,005DWT) also arrived in ballast from the Bristol Channel after delivering a cargo of granite to Yelland, North Devon from Glensanda, Scotland. The former **Arklow Rose** at the time of writing is still part of the Cardiff based Charles M.Willie (Shipping) Limited linking the United Kingdom to Iberia.

On 22nd January 2018 the **Baltica Hav** (1984, 1,762DWT) swings at Teignmouth prior to berthing astern of the **Eems Delta** (1992, 1,739DWT) which had arrived with a cargo of aggregates from Belfast. Both ships were British owned in the 1990s with the **Eems Delta** being launched as the **Torrent** for Franco-British Chartering Agency and was the last of the Yorkshire Dry Dock series of economy coasters that were popular with British owners from the early 1980s. The **Eems Delta** is now operating in West Africa as **Am Delta** and hit the headlines when hijacked by pirates off Nigeria in November 2020. The **Baltica Hav** was well known as **Union Pluto** and **Pluto** in the south east of England aggregate trade but is now sailing further afield with her new owners. The vessel was built by Hugo Peters of Wewelsfleth, Germany as yard no 602.

On 16th February 2018 the inbound **Eems Carrier** (1996, 2,200DWT) approaches Teignmouth from Southampton to load ball clay for Bendorf, Germany via Rotterdam. The low air draught coaster designed for operating on the inland waterways of Europe is managed by Amasus Shipping, a Dutch specialist in river-sea shipping with a fleet of 77 ships under its control in 2022. The vessel was built in the Netherlands by Scheepswerf Peters BV of Kampen as the **Koerier** and its arrival shows that for a few weeks each year it is possible to get the sun rising behind a ship approaching Teignmouth. Unfortunately, clear mornings, high tides and shipping movements rarely coincide.

On 24th March 2018 the **Fluvius Teign** (2005, 3,680DWT) arrives at Teignmouth from Hull with a cargo of rape seed meal. This was the first and only visit by this Exe Shipping vessel to her namesake river. Exe Shipping is based in Powderham and was formed in 2010 with all its vessels named after West Country rivers. To my knowledge there have only been four commercial vessels named after the Teign. Along with the **Fluvius Teign** there was the tug **Teign** that operated at Teignmouth until 1924, **Teignbank** a large now scrapped Bank Line vessel and the Teignmouth tug **Teign C** seen to the left. In November 2021 the vessel was sold to Danish owners and is now trading as the **Hanne**.

On 30th April 2018 the **Veendijk** (2009, 4,891DWT) departs from Teignmouth with a part cargo of ball clay. The vessel is heading to Fowey where she will top up with china clay before heading onward to Varna, Bulgaria. The impressive red hulled mini-bulker is one of around 20 vessels managed by Shipping Company Groningen, which was founded in 1996. To sail from Teignmouth to Fowey gave the crew the treat of visiting two of the most scenic ports in Europe.

On 19th May 2018 *Ferry No.4* (1946) is seen at Shaldon before crossing to Teignmouth. The Union flag was being carried to mark the Royal Wedding between Prince Harry and Meghan Markle taking place on this day. The Teignmouth to Shaldon ferry can be traced back to 1298 and still provides a daily service enjoyed by tourists and locals. The black and white gunports were added to the rowing boat ferries after the Napoleonic wars to make them look like Men o War. This tradition continued with the advent of the first motor ferries nos. 1 & 2 in 1907-08.

On 20th May 2018 the mini bunker *Spanaco Loyalty* (2007, 5,000DWT) arrives at a misty Teignmouth in ballast from Falmouth after dry docking. The former *Eileen C* was previously owned by Carisbrooke Shipping of Cowes and was built in Spain by Constructions Navales, P. Freire S.A. of Vigo.

On 29th June 2018 the **Zeeland** (2010, 3,609DWT) departs from Teignmouth for Figueira Da Foz, Portugal with a cargo of ball clay. The Dutch owned ship was built in the Czech Republic by Lodenice Nova Melnik and had recently been renamed from **Elane** when the picture was taken. The Back Beach pubs in Teignmouth appear to be doing very good business. On the right can be seen the tower of the Church of St Michael The Archangel built in 1821.

On 28th July 2018 the Teignmouth Harbour Commissioners tug **Teign C** stands in for the pilot boat **Syd Hook** at Teignmouth. The **Beaumotion** (2003, 3,836DWT) can be seen arriving from Belfast with a cargo of road stone. Both vessels are products of the prolific family owned Dutch ship builder Damen which now has over 30 yards worldwide. This photograph was taken from Shaldon Beach which provides excellent views of ships arriving and departing with the best light from lunch time onwards.

On 5th August 2018 Teignmouth held the annual Lifeboat Sunday event. The relief Severn Class All Weather Lifeboat 17-27 RNLB **Volunteer Spirit** (2001) visited from Brixham and entertained the crowds with a display close to the sea front promenade. The Severn class lifeboat is the largest lifeboat in the RNLI fleet developed in the early 1990s and introduced into the fleet in 1996. As an all-weather lifeboat, the Severn can take on the worst sea conditions on long offshore searches and rescues. The lifeboat is designed to lie afloat, either at deep-water moorings or alongside at a berth. Following an RNLI tradition of naming modern lifeboats after rivers, the Severn is named after the Severn River, the longest river in the UK. 46 of the class were built between 1992 and 2005 and a life extension program is currently underway to extend the life by another 25 years.

On 7th September 2018 the *Forseti* (1993, 3,574DWT) arrives at Teignmouth in ballast from Shoreham as the attractive wooden pleasure boat *Summer Wine* departs for an evening fishing trip. Built on the River Danube in Budapest, Hungary by the Ganz Danubus Shipyard & Machine Factory as the *Hornsund* the coaster is now operated by Latvian interests. Forseti is the god of justice and reconciliation in Norse mythology.

On 23rd September 2018 the Dutch **Eems Sun** (2009, 2,600DWT) departs from Teignmouth in ballast for Santander, Spain. After a lot of rain the port took advantage of a dry Sunday and discharged the ship for departure on the evening tide. Many European ship owners have looked east to reduce the cost of new ships. In this book there are examples of vessels from Bangladesh, China and India with this ship being built in Vietnam by Hong Ha Shipbuilding, Haiphong as Yard No.6.

On 13th November 2018 the Dutch built tug **Annamone** (1949) is seen above Shaldon Bridge whilst engaged on survey work on the bridge. A previous survey had found that some of the pillars on the bridge were formed of wood rather than the specified concrete. The wood had started to decay and a 3.5 tonne weight limit was imposed causing severe logistical problems for Shaldon whilst the pillars were rebuilt. The **Annamone** is owned by TMS Maritime Limited and is based on the River Teign between contracts. The tug joined the fleet in 2003 and is fitted with a 300hp John Deere main engine which creates a bollard pull of 3.5 tonnes. Previously the vessel was based in Leigh in Essex where it was registered as Maldon fishing vessel MN108 and was originally used as a ferry in the Netherlands.

On 20th November 2018 the Dutch owned **Panda** (2001, 2,953DWT) arrives at Teignmouth from Amsterdam in rough conditions with a cargo of animal feed. The river-sea ship is a Combo Porter 150 B type with a hull constructed in the Czech Republic and the vessel completed at the Kampen, Netherlands yard of Scheepswerf Peters BV. Like many Dutch coasters the vessel is always smartly turned out and whilst named **Panda** it carried a painted panda under the bridge. In December 2021 the vessel was renamed **Amadeus Diamond** still under the Dutch flag.

On 20th November 2018 the **Swedica Hav** (1986, 2,276DWT) arrives at Teignmouth after a long journey from Plymouth. Having not been able to get into Teignmouth due to the sea conditions the vessel had been crossing Lyme Bay to keep out of the worst of the weather. Another low air draught river-sea ship built by Peters of Wewelsfleth, Germany the vessel has previously carried the names **Jan Meeder**, **Sea Weser** and **Ophir** before joining the fleet of Hav Shipping in 2006.

On 14th December 2018 the river-sea ship **Leine** (2005, 2,928DWT) arrives at Teignmouth from Brugge with a cargo of animal feed. Built by Slovenske Lodenice A.S. of Komarno, Slovakia the vessel is currently trading as the **Elbetal**. Like many vessels visiting Teignmouth this vessel is fitted with a bridge mounted on a hydraulic platform so it can be lowered when passing under fixed structures on canals and rivers.

The rising sun on the morning of 9th January 2019 lights the **Wilson Ems** (1995, 1,536DWT) as it arrives at Teignmouth with a cargo from Schiedam, Holland. Wilson Ship Management is a Norwegian company with over 100 vessels, ranging from 1,500 to 8,500DWT and the light blue vessels regularly visit Teignmouth. The **Wilson Ems** was built by CSPL a.s. Chvaletice in the Czech Republic and is the baby of the Wilson fleet but should have made money on this trip as it reloaded ball clay for Rotterdam.

On 15th February 2019 the **Eems Coast** (1985, 1,490DWT) departs from Teignmouth for Rotterdam with a cargo of clay. Launched as the **Galaxa** at Scheepswerf 'Ferus Smit' BV of Westerbroek the vessel is still Dutch owned, registered and managed. In the background can be seen **Ferry No.5** which was built around 1973 originally for service in King's Lynn and is now the reserve ferry for the link across the Teign.

On 10th March 2019 a member of crew on **Elbetor** (1990, 3,432DWT) checks the hatches before departing from Teignmouth for orders. Built at Viana Do Castelo in Portugal as **Port Faro** for Portline the vessel was at the time of the photograph part of the large fleet operated by Strahlmann Reederi of Brunsbuttel, Germany but is now trading as the **Gulf Wind**.

On 16th April 2019 the **Paper Moon** (1990, 2,717DWT) departs from Teignmouth in ballast for Amsterdam. Built in Germany as the **Assidous** the vessel was owned by RTS Shipping Co. Ltd., Szczecin of Poland when operating to Teignmouth. The **Paper Moon** made 51 visits to Teignmouth, mostly carrying animal feed from Amsterdam and Rotterdam, before being sold for further trading in the Mediterranean with the economy name change to **Moon**. The ship was such a regular visitor that my eldest daughter made me laugh one day when we left to see a ship arriving and said, "I hope it is something more interesting than **Paper Moon**!" I am sure I am not the only one that misses the light blue hull on the quay.

On 4th May 2019 the Damen 2308 Shoalbuster multi-purpose tug **MTS Valour** (2006) arrives at Teignmouth with a barge from Greenock to be loaded with a crane for works in Brixham. The 23 tonne bollard pull tug is owned by Brixham based Marine and Towage Services and is part of a fleet of around 18 vessels that see service across Europe and further afield supporting infrastructure projects.

On 25th August 2019 the *Eems Solar* (2009, 2,530DWT) arrives at Teignmouth from Erith on the River Thames with a cargo of animal feed. The Dutch owned vessel was built by Shipbuilding-Haiphong of Vietnam and like many vessels visiting Teignmouth is registered in the north east Netherlands town of Delfzijl. Managed by Eems Werken of Werkendam, Netherlands it is one of around 20 short-sea vessels in the fleet which are a regular sight in Teignmouth.

On 1st December 2019 the **Christine** (1998, 4,743DWT) departs from Teignmouth for Plymouth. The ship was built by the Damen Shipyard in Hoogezand, Netherlands as the **Christina** and is seen crossing the sand bar at the entrance of the port from the Ness at Shaldon. Although tree growth in recent decades has limited the photographic opportunities the steep climb up the Ness headland is still rewarded with a magnificent panorama of Lyme Bay.

On 12th March 2020 the **Celtic Navigator** (2003, 4,327DWT) arrives at Teignmouth past the Fish Quay from Workington to load ball clay for Aveiro. The vessel built by Royal Bodewes of the Netherlands was making its first visit to Teignmouth as part of the Cardiff based Charles M. Willie (Shipping) Limited fleet which it joined in 2019 having previously carried the names **Almadiep**, **MTL Kouris** and **Modulus 4**.

On 29th March 2020 the Peel, Isle of Man registered *Vitality* (2009, 4,184DWT) departs from Teignmouth in ballast for the French Atlantic port of Les Sables-d'Olonne. Built by Rong Cheng Shipbuilding in China as the *Allerdiep* the vessel was at the time a recent addition to the Faversham Ships fleet and was still carrying the black hull of her previous owners before a repaint into the corporate blue of the East Cowes based owners.

On 4th April 2020 the **Moseldijk** (2009, 4,927DWT) departs from Teignmouth for Fowey where the cargo of ball clay will be topped up before sailing to Izmir, Turkey. The Shipping Company Groningen managed mini-bulker had recently been repainted in the striking red livery and made a fine sight departing on a lovely day. The relatively large vessel takes the tight 90 degree turn at the entrance of the harbour with ease.

On 18th April 2020 the **Paper Moon** (1990, 2,717DWT) departs from Teignmouth for Rotterdam to collect another load of animal feed. This picture shows her 50th departure from Teignmouth. In the background can be seen Teignmouth seafront and the sea wall which carries the London to Penzance railway above the beach. This is one of the few railway routes in the world where regular passengers check the tide times when planning train trips as a high sea can cause disruption to services.

On 4th May 2020 the 1959 built fishing vessel *Helen Claire* arrives at Teignmouth. Built in France the Brixham registered boat is based in Teignmouth and a regular sight in the estuary.

On the same day, the 1969 built wooden crabber *La Vagabonde Des Mers* arrives at Teignmouth to unload a catch. The Teignmouth fishing fleet benefits from a £1.1m fish quay which in 2016 replaced the previous wooden structure. Not only has the new quay improved fish landing facilities but a floating pontoon has also been provided to improve access for leisure and dive boats. It is also still a very popular place for children of all ages to fish for crabs.

On 6th May 2020 there was the rare sight of two Arklow ships in Teignmouth at the same time. The **Arklow Clan** (2017, 5,094DWT) departs from Teignmouth in ballast for Southampton as the **Arklow Rival** (2006, 4,933DWT) is seen on the quay. Dutch builder Ferus Smit's Westerbroek Yard completed the **Arklow Clan** as the fourth in a series of 10 open-hatch, single-deck, ice-classed cargo carriers, It is reported the 'C Class' vessel cost US$5.97 million to build and is fitted with a single MaK 6M25 engine providing a speed of approximately 11 knots.

On 7th May 2020 the **Arklow Rival** (2006, 4,933DWT) leaves Teignmouth for Margate Roads where she awaited orders. The attractive 'R Class' are now the smallest and amongst the oldest ships in the Arklow fleet and are gradually being sold with only four of the original 13 vessels remaining in the Arklow fleet as at January 2022. In July 2021 the **Arklow Rival** became the **Fri Liepaja** joining four other former sister ships under the flag of Norway and can continue to be seen in northern Europe. Two other 'R Class' vessels joined the Charles M. Willie (Shipping) Limited fleet and visit Teignmouth as the **Celtic Freedom** and **Celtic Venture**.

On 26th May 2020 the **Beaumaiden** (2008, 3,800DWT) arrives at Teignmouth in ballast from Erith to load ball clay. Fellow Vertom vessel **Fokko Ukena** (2007, 3,627DWT) is already loading ball clay having previously arrived from Amsterdam loaded. The Dutch operators were founded in 1974 and now have interests in around 75 vessels. The name Vertom refers to its first vessel **Vera Tomson**.

On 17th June 2020 the **RMS Saimaa** (2005, 2,634DWT) arrives at Teignmouth from Rochefort, France. Lake Saimaa in Finland, after which the vessel is named, is linked by the Saimaa Canal to the Gulf of Finland near Vyborg, Russia. The Saimax specification details the maximum size and required equipment for ships using the canal. The maximum dimensions are a length of 82.5 metres and a beam of 12.6 metres, the dimensions of this vessel fit nicely at 80.1 metres by 12.4 metres.

On 17th June 2020 the **Blue Note** (2010, 5,203DWT) departs from Teignmouth for orders. This is one of the largest ships in deadweight capacity to be handled at Teignmouth for many years. The ship was built by Israel Shipyard Ltd of Haifa and delivered a cargo from Norrkoping, Sweden but was not fully loaded on arrival. Although the average deadweight vessel handled at the port is around 3,000 tonnes and 90 metre length overall, the individual records are 124 metre length overall, 5,861 deadweight tonnes and 5.75 metre draft.

On 23rd June 2020 the **Arctica Hav** (1984, 2,324DWT) arrives at Teignmouth. The vessel had delivered a cargo of aggregates from Porthoustock Quarry in Cornwall to Shoreham in Sussex then ran light to Teignmouth where she would load ball clay for Gdansk, Poland. Launched as the **Hansa** the vessel has also been named **Pinguin** and **Union Venus**. Despite being launched in the year I started photographing ships at Teignmouth this was the first time I had photographed this classic Peters built vessel.

On 5th July 2020 the **Arklow Flair** (2007, 4,950DWT) arrives at Teignmouth from Rotterdam past the Ness on a fine summer evening. Arklow Shipping of Ireland is a leading operator in the European short-sea shipping industry with a fleet of around 60 vessels. Formed in 1966 by three vessel owners in the East Coast town the company is known for its investment in new tonnage usually from Northern European yards and for the emerald green hulls that photograph so well. The ten 'F Class' vessels are now amongst the smallest in the fleet which has grown in carrying capacity to benefit from the economies of scale with the largest ships having a carrying capacity of over 33,000 tonnes.

On 25th July 2020 the **Queen Victoria** (2007, 90,746GT) is seen at anchor at Labrador Bay, Teignmouth with the vehicle carrier **Wisdom Ace** (2013, 19,227DWT). The **Queen Victoria** was the first Cunard ship to lay-up off Teignmouth during the Covid-19 crisis after other Carnival Group vessels had been using the local waters since June 2020. The **Wisdom Ace**, which has the capacity to move 5,198 cars, spent a number of weeks awaiting orders as vehicle production and demand was impacted by COVID-19 shutdowns.

On 3rd August 2020 the coaster *Tejo Alges* (2001, 4,247DWT) departs from Teignmouth in ballast for Belfast. I believe this was the first time the vessel had visited Teignmouth and was unusual as it flies the flag of Portugal. In the foreground is the Lucette light that was constructed in 1953 following a bequest of £1,500 from Mrs Louis Lucette of Staffordshire in memory of her husband and many happy holidays in Teignmouth. A few weeks after this picture was taken the Bulgarian built coaster suffered an engine room fire in the Bay of Biscay on 1st September 2020. The fire was successfully extinguished by the crew but as a result the vessel was disabled and drifted until a tug towed the the vessel back to El Ferrol, Spain.

At the sunrise on 2nd September 2020 the **Queen Mary 2** (2003, 149,215GT) arrives at Teignmouth to lay up during the COVID-19 pandemic. The last ocean liner is usually employed linking Hamburg and Southampton with New York and is specially designed for all year-round crossings of the North Atlantic. In the foreground is Teignmouth Grand Pier, which was built between 1865 and 1867 to a design by J.W. Wilson. One of only two remaining piers on the South West coast of England it originally had a landing stage at the end for steamer services but this was removed in the 1960s. Today the family-owned pier still provides entertainment for all the family despite a regular battering from the sea, including in 2014 when 90% of the machines were lost and the pier suffered considerable damage that resulted in six months' closure.

On 9th September 2020 the **Queen Mary 2** (2003, 149,215GT) is seen with the **Elandra Denali** (2020, 299,999DWT). The very large crude carrier had unusually been chartered for its maiden voyage to carry a cargo of Korean jet fuel. With a shortage of storage capacity the tanker spent a number of months at anchor in Lyme Bay waiting for the market to improve.

On 29th September 2020 the Cunard ocean liner **Queen Mary 2** (2003, 149,215GT) stands at anchor awaiting orders as the coaster **Anton** (2010, 4,487DWT) heads into Teignmouth with a cargo of animal feed from Ghent. Launched as the **Karella** by the Omega Shipyard, Petrozavodsk, Russia, the arrival of the coaster the previous day had to be aborted due to insufficient water.

On 2nd October 2020 the CLdn roll-on roll-off ferry *Opaline* (2010, 13,439DWT) shelters from Storm Alex off Teignmouth whilst sailing from Rotterdam to Leixoes, Portugal. The 270 trailer capacity ferry was built in Flensburg, Germany and provides a sea-bridge service between Northern Europe and Portugal. Luxembourg based CLdN has roots dating back to 1928 and now operates over 140 sailings each week with a fleet of over 30 ferries serving 12 ports with over a million freight units moved every year.

On 7th October 2020 the Teignmouth Atlantic 85 lifeboat B-809 **The Two Annes** (2006) returns to the station. The first lifeboat was stationed at Teignmouth in 1851 but the station closed in 1950. 50 years later with increasing leisure use the lifeboat station reopened and the current lifeboat has been at Teignmouth since August 2006. The inshore lifeboat is kept in the original 1862 boathouse from which the volunteer crew undertake around 40 rescues every year.

On 28th October 2020 the *Naja* (1997, 3,526DWT) arrives at Teignmouth in ballast from Ipswich. In the background can be seen the reefer *Crown Opal* (1997, 10,316DWT) sheltering en route to Agadir, Morocco. The eagle eyed will also note a geared bulker *Aphrodite M* (2011, 34,399DWT) heading to Aratu, Brazil over the horizon. The *Naja* was the first ship fitted with cranes to arrive at Teignmouth for many years and this was believed to be the first visit by this ship. The *Naja* was built by Slovenske Lodenice A.S. of Komarno, Slovakia and in March 2021 transferred to the flag of Vanuatu with the new name *Anka Sky*.

On 28th October 2020 the **Queen Victoria** (2007, 90,746GT) joined big sister **Queen Mary 2** (2003, 149,215GT) at anchor off Maidencombe. In the background can be seen the bulk carrier **Amalea** (2008, 28,451DWT) sheltering en route to Abidjan, Ivory Coast and the multipurpose dry cargo heavy lift vessel **Henrik S** (2007, 11,169DWT), also sheltering whilst heading to Aliaga, Turkey.

On 25th November 2020 the P&O Grand-class sister ships **Azura** (2010, 115,055GT) and **Ventura** (2008, 116,017GT) are seen off Teignmouth whilst laid up during the COVID-19 pandemic lockdown. Both ships were built for the British market by Fincantieri in Monfalcone, Italy. The **Azura** was named by ballerina Dame Darcy Bussell and the **Ventura** by actress Dame Helen Mirren.

On 25th November 2020 the **Paper Star** (1989, 2,750DWT) departs from Teignmouth in ballast for Rotterdam as the **Syd Hook** transfers the pilot to the **Fluvius Otter** (1989, 3,193DWT) which is arriving from Amsterdam. Both vessels were engaged in the movement of animal feed which is the main import commodity at Teignmouth. The **Fluvius Otter** is operated by Devon based Exe Shipping and is named after the River Otter in East Devon. The vessel was originally delivered to Arklow Shipping by Barkmeijer Stroobos of the Netherlands as the **Arklow Spray** and it entered the Powderham based fleet in 2014.

The **Paper Star** is Polish owned and managed and following the sale of sister ship **Paper Moon** has remained a regular visitor to Teignmouth with imports of animal feed from Rotterdam and Amsterdam. The coaster was built for German owners by Rolandwerft Detlef Hegemann of Bremen, Germany as the **Antina** and visited the Teign eight times in 2021.

On 6th December 2020 the CLdn ro-ro ferry **Vespertine** (2010, 14,483DWT) is seen sheltering off Teignmouth whilst en route from Rotterdam to Leixoes. Earlier in 2020 the German built vessel had an additional deck added in Gdansk.

On the evening of 7th December 2020 the **Azura** (2010, 115,055GT), **Queen Elizabeth** (2010, 90,901GT), **Marella Discovery** (1996, 69,472GT) and **Queen Mary 2** (2003, 149,215GT) line up perfectly whilst at anchor off Maidencombe.

On 11th December 2020 the **Blue Star 1** (2005, 5,246DWT) is seen arriving at Teignmouth in ballast from Aveiro, Portugal. The vessel is a rare sight in Northern Europe being owned by Fetida Marine of the Ukraine and built in China at the Xiangshan Qianjin Shipyard, Zhejiang as the **Jing Fu Xing 22**. The tug **Teign C** was required to assist the large vessel as it is not fitted with a bow thruster.

On Christmas Day 2020 there was a spectacular sunrise. The laid up passenger ships **Ventura** (2008, 116,017GT) and **Queen Mary 2** (2003, 149,215GT) are seen off Maidencombe as the crews experience a Christmas Day like no other.

On 27th December 2020 the **MPI Resolution** (2003, 7,000DWT) sheltered off Teignmouth. The vessel was the first purpose built for installing wind farms and is fitted with a 600 tonne capacity main crane. To allow the vessel to self-elevate and create a 3,200 square metre work platform for installing wind turbines it has a jack up system using six legs each with a length 70.492 m.

On 10th January 2021 the *Figaro* (2003, 1,851DWT) built by the Peters Shipyard in Kampen, Netherlands is seen at Teignmouth having arrived in ballast from Renteria, Spain to load ball clay for Landskrona, Sweden. The river-sea ship is operated by Baltnautic Shipping of Klaipeda, Lithuania as part of a fleet numbering around 28 ships and is seen from the Ness headland at Shaldon.

On 22nd January 2021 the *Sea Harmony* (1991, 3,182DWT) departs from Teignmouth light for Rotterdam, Netherlands. The ship had arrived from Rouen, France with a cargo of agricultural products. Built at Viana Do Castelo in Portugal the coaster is managed by GT Gillie & Blair Limited of Newcastle Upon Tyne. Founded in 1911 as a ship owning company operating coastal bulk carriers mainly on coal trades it now has interests in around eight short sea vessels which are a common sight around the UK.

On 4th February 2021 the **Adele** (1991, 3,269DWT) arrives at Teignmouth in ballast from Rotterdam, Netherlands to load clay for Mjoesund. Sweden. Built by Estaleiros Navais Do Mondego in Figueira Da Foz, Portugal the vessel was launched as the **Medeur Secondo** and at the time of the photograph registered in Latvia and owned by Klip Marine of Estonia. In August 2021 the vessel was renamed **GT Vela** and registered under the flag of Antigua and Barbuda. The landing craft **MTS Terramare** can be seen at Polly Steps loading a 360-degree excavator and a mini dumper for the works on Dawlish sea wall.

On 5th February 2021 the 1980 Cornish built **Girl Rona** returns to Teignmouth with a catch of sprats. This is the second Teignmouth fishing boat to carry the name **Girl Rona** after the daughter of the owner, the late Reg Matthews. Alongside owning fishing boats Reg Matthews was also the harbour master at Teignmouth from 1978 to 2001 and a navigation light at Shaldon carries his name in recognition of his long service to the port.

On 6th February 2021 the **Queen Mary 2** (2003, 149,215GT), **Marella Explorer 2** (1995, 72,458GT), **Marella Discovery** (1996, 69,472GT), **Ventura** (2008, 116,017GT), **Queen Victoria** (2007, 90,746GT) and **Arcadia** (2005, 84,342GT) await orders off Teignmouth. This view is taken from the hills between Bishopsteignton and Teignmouth. The Teign estuary, Shaldon and the Ness can be seen in the foreground.

During lock down the sheltered waters of Lyme Bay and adjacent Tor Bay had up to ten passenger ships laid up from the fleets of the Carnival Corporation and TUI. The ships made regular trips away for stores, bunkers, water production and crew changes and when weather conditions deteriorated the vessels often moved for shelter including to Baie de la Seine, France. The good news is that as cruising activity tentatively recommenced in 2021 there was an increase in cruise visits to the area and it is hoped that this will continue in future years.

On 6th February 2021 the **Marella Discovery** (1996, 69,472GT), **Queen Mary 2** (2003, 149,215GT), **Marella Explorer 2** (1995, 72,458GT), **Queen Victoria** (2007, 90,746GT) and **Ventura** (2008, 116,017GT) await orders off Teignmouth.

On 22nd February 2021 the **Pregol Hav** (1985, 2,291DWT) arrives at Teignmouth light from Belfast to load ball clay for Bendorf, Germany. The end destination for the clay is on the River Rhine near Koblenz many miles from the sea. Oslo, Norway based Hav Shipping has a number of 1980s built river-sea ships in its fleet and they are regular visitors to Teignmouth often loading clay.

On 25th February 2021 the **Dutch Pearl** (2010, 254GT) tows the walking jackup platform **Wavewalker 1** away from Dawlish. Built at the Gebr. Kooiman Shipyard in Zwijndrecht the **Dutch Pearl** is a 31-metre long double propelled chine strake hull multipurpose tugboat with stern roll and push bow. The vessel has a bollard pull of 46.2 tonnes and can carry out its work in shallow as well as deep water. The **Wavewalker 1** was being returned to Newhaven having provided a platform for piling work on the sea wall at Dawlish.

On 26th February 2021 the Cunard flagship **Queen Mary 2** (2003, 149,215GT) is seen anchored off Maidencombe whilst laid up during the COVID-19 pandemic.

On 16th March 2021 the laid up passenger ships **Marella Explorer 2** (1995, 72,458GT) and **Ventura** (2008, 116,017GT) are joined by the Point Class roll on/roll off sealift vessel **Hurst Point** (2002, 13,274DWT) off Maidencombe. The latter vessel is on charter to the British Ministry of Defence from Foreland Shipping. With its three sisters the **Hurst Point** can regularly be seen in local waters usually awaiting its next task moving military equipment around the world. To illustrate the world wide use of these ships during July and August 2021 the **Hurst Point** visited Singapore, Oman, Kenya and Diego Garcia.

On 26th April 2021 the **Bonita** (1987, 1,469DWT) departs from Teignmouth loaded with ball clay for Rotterdam. The diminutive Latvian registered coaster had arrived in ballast from Rouen and was built by Ferus Smit Scheepswerf of Hoogezand, Netherlands as the **Laura II**. An excellent elevated view of ships departing in the evening is available from the Botanical Gardens in Shaldon. Now owned by the local authority the gardens were created by Maria Laetitia Kempe Homeyard in the late 1920s and early 1930s, and were built by Thomas Rider of Southwark, London and the designer William Sears.

On 15th May 2021 the **Queen Elizabeth** (2010, 90,901GT) and the **Arcadia** (2005, 84,342GT) stand off Teignmouth. This spectacular view of the Teign estuary is taken from the hills above the village of Bishopsteignton. Teignmouth can be seen in the foreground whilst on the far bank of the estuary can be seen Shaldon and the Ness. The tight turn into the port can be clearly seen.

On 26th May 2021 the P&O Grand-class ship *Ventura* (2008, 116,017GT) is seen off Teignmouth whilst laid up during the COVID-19 pandemic lockdown. With a capacity of 3,192 passengers, the ship was built by Fincantieri at its shipyard in Monfalcone, Italy.

On 27th May 2021 the Dutch coaster *Calypso* (2011, 3,796DWT) arrives at Teignmouth from Poole in ballast to load ball clay for Chioggia, Italy. The Rotterdam registered vessel was built in Bergum, Netherlands and carries the colours of the Netherlands national football team like many other coasters from the country. The mist on the River Teign is known as the Larry and when it coincides with a high tide it can provide some interesting photo opportunities.

On 29th May 2021 the **Danica Hav** (1984, 1,720DWT) arrives at Teignmouth with a cargo of road stone from Belfast. The vessel, built by Peters of Wewelsfleth, Germany, was having a few profitable days as it loaded ball clay in Teignmouth for Gdansk, Poland. An eastbound cargo from the UK can be hard to find so two was very good work by the agents.

The Cardiff registered *Celtic Mariner* (2001, 3,676DWT) departs from Teignmouth with a cargo of ball clay for Figueira da Foz, Portugal. Ball clay is quarried from the Bovey Basin which stretches from Newton Abbot to Bovey Tracey, approximately five miles from Teignmouth. The Bovey Basin is considered to have the biggest deposits of high quality ball clay in the world and it is exported to around 80 different countries. The name ball clay derives from the traditional method of winning the clay where it was cut from the floor of an open pit in cubes. After being handled the corners were knocked off and the clay turned into a ball by the time it was delivered to the potters.

On 13th June 2021 the **Aberdeen** (2009, 3,614DWT) arrives from Le Légué, France to load ball clay for Sfax, Tunisia, a loaded journey worth the ballast trip from France. The **Teign C** was acting as pilot boat whilst the **Syd Hook** was out of service.

On 24th June 2021 the **Regal Princess** (2014, 142,714GT) is seen anchored awaiting the resumption of cruising following the COVID-19 lock down. The **Dolfijn** (1989, 2,450DWT) arrives off Teignmouth to anchor having travelled light from Newport, South Wales to load clay for Gdansk, Poland. Delivered by Gebr. Buys Scheepsbouw of Krimpen a/d Ijssel, Netherlands the front section of the coaster's hull was built by Scheepswerf Slob, Papendrecht, Netherlands. Unusually the vessel has carried the same name since she was launched.

On 12th July 2021 the **Arlecchino** (1995, 2,503DWT) arrives at Teignmouth with a cargo of road stone from Belfast. The vessel was launched as the **Boeran** at Scheepswerf Bijlsma BV of Wartena, Netherlands and when named **RMS Rahm** was a fairly regular visitor to Teignmouth. The Ness sandstone headland on the Shaldon side of the estuary forms the prominent backdrop.

On 18th July 2021 the smart Dutch river-sea ship **Ashley** (2000, 2,800DWT) arrives at Teignmouth from Dordrecht, Netherlands. The Combi Porter 1450 type was completed by Peters Shipyard in Kampden, Netherlands with the hull supplied by Lodonice Krescice of Decin, Czech Republic. The sea safari boat **Whistler** can be seen departing on a trip to see local marine life.

On 16th July 2021 the dredger **Mannin** (1972, 209DWT) was working on The Point at Teignmouth. The dredger operated by Padstow Harbour Commissioners is a regular sight in Teignmouth and was built by J.W. Cook & Co. of Wivenhoe, Essex for service in the Isle of Man. It generally takes around 40 minutes to load a cargo of 100 cubic metres and five minutes to discharge it through opening bottom doors. At Teignmouth the dredged sand is usually discharged locally off Sprey Point to replenish the beach. During 2021 the **Mannin** was under overhaul at Polruan, Cornwall for an extended period and it was a welcome sight back at work clearing the channel at Teignmouth.

On 27th July 2021 all four berths at Teignmouth are full as are the two berths on the Fish Quay. The **Gala Trio** (1993, 2,767DWT) leads the line up of four ships as she awaits her turn to load having run from Ostend anchorage to load for Castellon, Spain. **RMS Wanheim** (1990, 2,620DWT) is next loading clay for Finland, the **GT Auriga** (1993, 3,582DWT) is discharging agricultural bulk products from Amsterdam and closest is Faversham Shipping's latest acquisition **Conformity** (2007, 3,859DWT) which arrived in mid-July from Amsterdam with agricultural bulks.

On 23rd August 2021 the trip boat **Restless** takes an evening excursion up the River Teign into Newton Abbot. Built in Teignmouth in 1965 by Stanley Hook, Syd Hook and Jim Belton the boat is passing along a section of river that linked the Stover Canal to the estuary and in years gone by saw the transport on barges of Dartmoor granite and ball clay to the ships at Teignmouth. Now operated by Riviera Cruises, the **Restless** with William Hook (Bill) as the Coxswain was used as an Auxiliary Lifeboat for many years until the RNLI reopened Teignmouth lifeboat station.

On 28th August 2021 the **Mia Sophie-B** (1995, 2,300DWT) arrives at Teignmouth with a cargo of ground granulated blast furnace slag (GGBS) from Port Talbot. The local pilot gig **Nessie** waits for her to clear the channel. The **Mia Sophie-B** was built by Schiffswerft Bodenwerder of Germany as the **Tulos** for Russian interests as one of the eight ship 'Vyg Type'. Rowing is a very popular pastime on the estuary with the 1994 formed River Teign Rowing Club now one of the biggest rowing clubs in the UK with the gigs and traditional Seine boats out on the water throughout the year.

GGBS is a by-product of steel making and is obtained by quenching molten iron slag to produce a glassy, granular product. This is then dried and ground into a highly cementitious fine powder for use as a substitute for Portland cement. Because GGBS is a by-product its manufacture requires less than one third of the energy and produces less than 10% of the CO_2 emissions of Portland cement. Teignmouth receives regular shipments from Port Talbot in South Wales where the enclosed dock was reopened in 1998 to allow the loading of GGBS direct to coastal vessels for delivery to customers around the UK for use in concrete.

On 3rd September 2021 the top sail schooner *Johanna Lucretia* (1946) arrives at Teignmouth to take part in the Maritime and Shanty Festival. Built in Ghent as a fishing vessel it is now based in Plymouth as a sail training vessel.

On 6th September 2021 the **RMS Twisteden** (2002, 2,688DWT) departs from Teignmouth in ballast for Aviles, Spain having delivered road stone from Belfast. In October 2021 it was announced that Norwegian operator Wilson AS would acquire six vessels and the contract portfolio from Rhenus Maritime Services (RMS). Wilson will also take on a short-term lease from RMS up to six dry bulk carriers.

On 6th September 2021 the **Celtic Forester** (2003, 4,323DWT) catches the last of the sun as it arrives into Teignmouth with road salt from Kilroot, Northern Ireland. Started in 1965 by three Irish American brothers, the Irish Salt Mining & Exploration Co. Ltd, operates one of only three salt mines in the UK. Based three miles north east of Carrickfergus on the northern shore of Belfast Lough, the company produces around 500,000 tonnes of de-icing rock salt per annum and

has its own deep-water berth. In recent years local authorities have made more use of Teignmouth to import salt rather than using road transport from ports outside the county.

On 23rd September 2021 the **Wings** (1989, 3,432DWT) arrives at Teignmouth in ballast from Poole to load ball clay for Gdansk, Poland. The ship had delivered timber to Poole from Ventspils, Latvia and then picked up a very convenient reload to the Baltic. The vessel was built in Portugal as the **Port Lima** and was part of the German operator Reederei Erwin Strahlmann fleet as the **Burgtor** until renamed earlier in 2021.

On 23rd September 2021 the **Lyrika** (1994, 2,350DWT) leaves Teignmouth with a cargo of ball clay for Vyborg, Russia. The **Riwal** (1992, 3,735DWT) is already in the channel arriving in ballast from Ellesmere Port to load ball clay for Alexandria, Egypt. Launched as the **Priwall** the inbound coaster is a product of Slovenske Lodenice A.S. of Slovakia whilst the Lithuanian owned **Lyrika** was built by Peters of Kampen, Netherlands as yard no.436.

On 25th October 2021 Teignmouth has four coasters alongside. From right to left is the **Spanaco Fidelity** (2009, 4,192DWT) which had arrived from Lillebonne, France. The **Fri Ocean** (2000, 3,640DWT) is astern having arrived from Rostock, Germany. The diminutive **Bonita** (1987, 1,470DWT) had arrived from Rotterdam and like the previous two vessels delivered agricultural bulks. Last in the line-up is **Shetland Trader** (1992, 2,386DWT) which had delivered road stone from Belfast. There are working quays of 119 metres and 300 metres which are able to accommodate four vessels of suitable length as seen here. The cargo handling is supported by 14,000 square metres of warehousing and extensive quayside storage.

On 10th November 2021 the **Amadeus Silver** (2011, 2,570DWT) is seen at Teignmouth having arrived in ballast from Saint Brieuc, France. The vessel was delivered to Union Transport of Bromley, Kent as the **Union Silver**, a fleet of ships that were a regular sight in Teignmouth through the 1980s and 1990s. Astern the **Bonay** (1991, 1,891DWT) is seen after arriving from Great Yarmouth with grain.

The next generation...